D0529254

WORLD RECORD BREAKERS

THE WORLD'S FASTEST CARS

BY SEAN MCCOLLUM

Consultant:
Leslie Mark Kendall, Curator
Petersen Automotive Museum
Los Angeles, California, USA

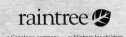
raintree
a Capstone company — publishers for children

Raintree is an imprint of Capstone Global Library Limited, a company incorporated in England and Wales having its registered office at 264 Banbury Road, Oxford, OX2 7DY – Registered company number: 6695582

www.raintree.co.uk
myorders@raintree.co.uk

Edited by Mandy Robbins
Designed by Sarah Bennett
Picture research by Morgan Walters
Production by Laura Manthe
Printed and bound in China.

ISBN 978-1-4747-1159-3
21 20 19 18 17
10 9 8 7 6 5 4 3 2 1

British Library Cataloguing in Publication Data
A full catalogue record for this book is available from the British Library.

Acknowledgements
We would like to thank the following for permission to reproduce photographs: Shutterstock: Alta Oosthuizen, 18, Amee Cross, Cover, Audrey Snider-Bell, top 23, DEmax, deAlamy: PhotoKratky, 14; Corbis: Skyscan, 25; Getty Images: Sports Studio Photos, 12; Newscom: Hennessey/Splash News, 10, Jeff Speer/Icon Sportswire CEO, 18, Tim Scott/Fluid Images/ REX, spread 4-5, Zdenko Hirschler/REX, 28; Shutterstock: Claudio Del Luongo, bottom 27, DEmax, design element, Dong liu, 8, Eky Studio, design element, FotoYakov, design element, HodagMedia, 13, spread 16-17, Joshua Rainey Photography, 23, Lissandra Melo, top 27, Max Earey, 9, Patrick Poendl, spread 6-7, Phillip Rubino, 20, 21, Seraphim Art, design element, Steve Mann, 26, Wiktoria Pawlak, design element, YuryKo, 11, ZRyzner, cover

CONTENTS

TO THE MAX

Every August, hundreds of fast-car fans travel to Bonneville Salt Flats in Utah, USA, for Speed Week. Drivers take advantage of the hard, flat surface to test their cars' top speed. Classic hot rods, dragsters, bullet-shaped experimental cars and more all take their turns. The drivers have just one goal – to see how fast they can go. Speed Week has become a legendary event for lovers of powerful cars.

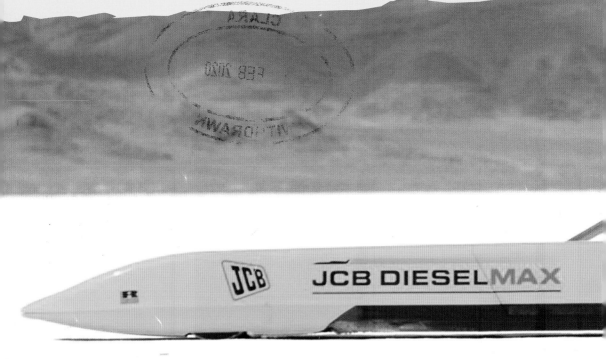

Since the first car was shifted into gear in the 1800s, drivers have wanted to test the limits of speed. Car designers and engineers have built powerful engines. They have bolted them into sleek bodies. Carmakers test their ideas on racetracks. They build high-performance sports cars, or "supercars", that travel on public roads. A few design vehicles powered by jet or rocket engines in hopes of winning the land speed record.

These car enthusiasts share a passion. They love the thrill of going fast, faster and fastest. They experiment with every detail in order to squeeze extra speed out of four-wheeled machines.

The *Dieselmax* streamliner blazes down the Bonneville Salt Flats in 2006.

CHAPTER 1

SUPERCARS

Cars of every size and shape zip along the world's roads. Many people want vehicles that are **reliable** and inexpensive. Speed and looks aren't as important to them.

Some drivers, though, want something flashier and much faster. Many of these supercars look like something from a science fiction film. Carmakers such as Bugatti, Porsche and Koenigsegg produce only a small number of supercar models. Supercars must be street legal. That means they meet all the safety needs of normal road vehicles. But they blow away all the standards of speed and style.

FACT

In 2015 the Ford Fiesta was the most popular factory-made car in the United Kingdom. It can speed to 169 kilometres (105 miles) per hour. That is less than half the speed of the fastest supercar, the Hennessey Venom GT.

reliable steady, dependable

POWER AND WEIGHT

What makes a car fast? The key is the combination of power and weight. A powerful engine is important. But the less weight the engine has to move, the faster the car can go. Supercar makers use lightweight materials. Many supercar frames and bodies are built mostly of carbon fibre. This material is stronger than steel yet weighs a lot less. It is also easy to mould. It can be formed into shapes that slice through the air. Other features help the cars grip the road.

The Porsche 911 Carrera on display in 2011

911 Carrera

Supercars push the limits of speed and **engineering**. The makers test new technologies that can help make all cars better and safer. Check out three of the world's fastest supercars.

FAST: KOENIGSEGG AGERA

Since he was a boy, Christian von Koenigsegg loved working on machines. He also dreamed of building cool cars. As a young man, he made his dream come true. His car company, Koenigsegg, develops and builds supercars. Between 2010 and 2015, the Koenigsegg company built several models of the Agera. The Agera RS engine has a whopping 1,160 **horsepower**. It can **accelerate** from 0 to 60 miles (97 kilometres) in 2.5 seconds. The car's estimated top speed is 402 kilometres (250 miles) per hour. The company continues to design newer models to go even faster.

A Koenigsegg Agera R on display in 2012

engineering design and construction

horsepower unit for measuring an engine's power

accelerate increase speed

FASTER: BUGATTI VEYRON 16.4 SUPER SPORT

Bugatti built only 30 of the stylish Veyron 16.4 Super Sports in 2010. Drivers snapped them up even though the price tag was £1.7 million. The Super Sport's engine cranks out 1,200 horsepower. It can go from 0 to 60 miles (97 kilometres) per hour in 2.5 seconds. The Veyron 16.4 Super Sport set a Guinness World Record for the fastest road car. It blasted to a top speed of 431 kilometres (267.8 miles) per hour. At such high speeds, the car's rear wing and other features automatically adjust. These shifts make the car more stable on the road.

The Bugatti Veyron Super Sport shows its power on mountain roads in Spain in 2010.

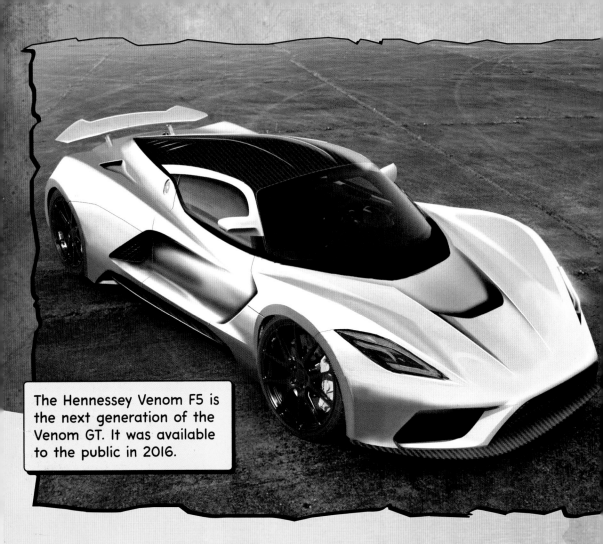

The Hennessey Venom F5 is the next generation of the Venom GT. It was available to the public in 2016.

FASTEST: HENNESSEY VENOM GT

The Venom GT's front end looks like a snake's head. In 2014 builders tested this Texas, USA-built supercar on a NASA runway. It hit 435 kilometres (270.49 miles) per hour. Its twin-turbocharger V-8 engine and sleek shape made that speed possible. John Hennessey heads the company that built the Venom GT. He called it "the supercar I have always dreamed of building." Each one costs £850,500.

WORDS OF POWER

Carmakers use special terms for what makes cars growl and go.
Learn the meanings of some car-related terms.

turbocharger and supercharger	These devices crank up the engine's power. They force extra air into the engine's cylinders. There, it is mixed with fuel and squeezed, or compressed. The explosive mix is then lit by a spark plug.
torque	This is the force used to rotate an object. For cars, torque usually describes their power to accelerate.
revolutions per minute (RPMs)	RPMs tell how hard the engine is working. They measure how fast an engine's crankshaft is turning. The crankshaft transfers power from the engine to its drive train and wheels.
engine displacement	This measures the amount of air an engine uses. For example, the 2015 Venom GT has a 7.0-litre engine. That means it sucks in and blows out 1.8 gallons (7.0 litres) of air with each full turn of the engine's crankshaft. Generally, the higher the number, the more powerful the engine.

FACT

Scottish inventor James Watt first used the term horsepower in the 1700s. He compared the amount of work a steam engine could do to work done by a strong horse.

CHAPTER 2

ON THE RACECOURSE

The first Indy 500 was held in the United States in 1911. Ray Harroun won the race with an average speed of 121 kilometres (75 miles) per hour. His car looked like a metal coffin on wheels. More than 100 years later, IndyCars look like fighter jets. Practice laps at Indianapolis Motor Speedway in Indiana, USA, can reach 370 kilometres (230 miles) per hour. That's three times faster than the race's first champion car.

Ray Harroun speeds to victory at the 1911 Indy 500.

High-performance race cars are designed and built with chest-thumping power. But straight-ahead speed might be only one factor in creating a fast car. Some race cars also need to grip the track and handle curves. They may need to be sturdy enough to not break down while racing hundreds or even thousands of kilometres. They must be strong and safe enough to protect drivers during a crash.

The fastest race cars on oval tracks and winding racecourses are sports cars, stock cars and **open-wheelers**. Each class has its own strict rules. These rules are meant to promote safety and competition. But they do not limit the thrills of powerful cars battling at super-high speeds.

IndyCars today look quite different than those from 1911.

open-wheeler race car built with the wheels outside of the main body; F1 cars and IndyCars are open-wheelers

SPORTS CARS

Sports cars are seen on public roads and on racetracks. They excel in endurance races, such as the 24 Hours of Daytona in Florida, USA. In professional sports car races like this one, there are two main classes: prototypes and grand touring (GT) cars. Prototypes are designed for racing. GTs are supposed to be more like production models that anyone can buy. On **straights**, prototype sports cars top 322 kilometres (200 miles) per hour or more. GTs are only a little slower.

FACT

The 24 Hours of Le Mans is a relay race that lasts for 24 hours. Each car has more than one driver. Cars keep going rain or shine, in daylight and through the night. The car that covers the most distance wins.

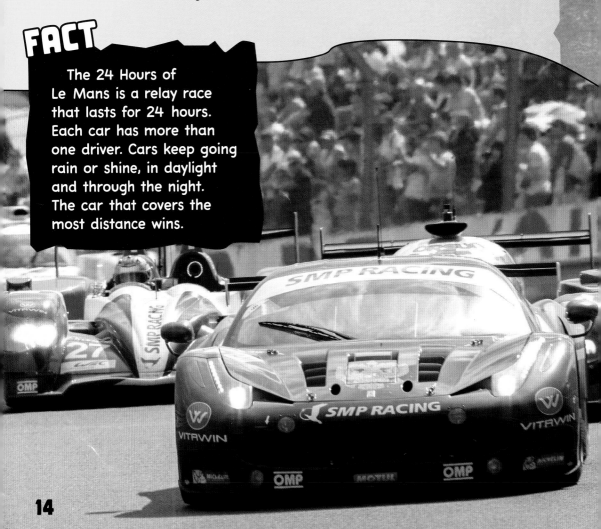

France's 24 Hours of Le Mans is a supreme test for sports cars. The racecourse is about 13.7 kilometres (8.5 miles) long. It includes tight corners and small hills. To win, a car needs to be more than just fast. It must quickly get in and out of sharp turns. It needs to be tough enough to handle more than 4,828 kilometres (3,000 miles) of hard driving.

STOCK CARS

Until about 1960, most stock cars on the racetracks were regular road vehicles. Drivers tuned up their factory models and raced. Today, though, stock cars are carefully designed power-monsters.

Stock cars must meet strict rules for power and weight. Engines can be about 725 horsepower. In some races the cars must use **carburetor** restrictor plates. The plates cut horsepower in half. They are meant to improve safety and competition by reducing speeds. Even with the plates, top stock cars can run laps that average 306 kilometres (190 miles) per hour or more.

straights long, straight part of a racetrack between turns; cars reach their highest speeds on the straights

carburetor engine part that mixes air and fuel

INDYCARS AND FORMULA 1

IndyCar engines are limited to about 650 horsepower. That is less power than a stock car engine. So why are IndyCars faster? The answer is weight. On oval speedways, IndyCars can weigh only 714 kilograms (1,575 pounds). Stock cars that race in NASCAR events must weigh 1,497 kilograms (3,300 pounds). That is more than twice as heavy as an IndyCar.

The combination of powerful engines, lightweight cars and wind-cutting **aerodynamics** makes IndyCars fast. In fact, they are considered the fastest cars on the world's curved racetracks. Top speeds average 370 kilometres (230 miles) per hour during practice laps on large oval speedways.

FACT

The downforce created by IndyCars is so strong they could drive on an upside-down racetrack.

aerodynamics science of how objects move through air

IndyCars speed around the track at a 2014 race in Wisconsin, USA.

Formula 1 (F1) cars look a lot like IndyCars, but they are smaller, lighter and not quite as fast. They are popular in the United Kingdom, Europe and other parts of the world. The top speeds of F1 cars are about 8 kilometres (5 miles) per hour slower than IndyCars.

WHY FAST CARS HAVE WINGS

Rushing air can make fast cars unstable at high speeds. They may lose grip on the road or track and spin out of control. They can even flip into the air.

That is why open-wheelers and some other race cars have airfoils. These car parts are shaped like aeroplane wings. The big difference is that they are put on upside down. They push the car down onto the track. This downforce helps the car stay on the ground. It also gives drivers more control of the vehicle.

CHAPTER 3

ON THE DRAG STRIP

Tony Schumacher inched his front wheels to the starting line and stopped. His eyes locked on the pole of starting lights known as the "Christmas tree". The lights lit up – yellow, yellow, yellow, GREEN! Flames erupted from the rear engine of Schumacher's Top Fuel dragster. Less than 4 seconds later he was 305 metres (1,000 feet) away and celebrating. He was the first drag racer to go faster than 531 kilometres (330 miles) per hour in a race.

Pro racer Tony Schumacher takes off down the drag strip.

When it comes to fast cars, nothing roars like dragsters. They are the fire-breathing dragons of straight-line speed. They specialize in instant acceleration down a straight racetrack. Since they don't have to slow down to negotiate turns, dragsters can reach mind-blowing speeds. The fastest can go from 0 to 300 miles (482 kilometres) per hour in less than 4 seconds.

There are many types of dragsters. But three types dominate the sport in National Hot Rod Association pro drag racing: Top Fuel, Funny Cars and Pro Stock dragsters.

	TYPE OF DRAGSTER		
	TOP FUEL	FUNNY CAR	PRO STOCK
Length	7.6 metres (25 feet)	5.5 metres (18 feet)	4.6 metres (about 15 feet)
Weight	1,052 kilograms (2,320 pounds)	1,043 kilograms (2,300 pounds)	1,066 kilograms (2,350 pounds)
Approximate horsepower	10,000	8,000	1,300
Top speeds	531 kilometres (330 miles) per hour	531 kilometres (330 miles) per hour	338 kilometres (210 miles) per hour
Fuel	**nitromethane**	nitromethane	racing gasoline

nitromethane mix of nitric acid and propane gas used as fuel in some dragsters

PRO STOCK

Pro Stock dragsters look a little bit like factory made cars. But their huge front air scoop hints at something wicked under the bonnet. The fastest Pro Stock cars reach speeds of at least 338 kilometres (210 miles) per hour. In 2014 Erica Enders-Stevens set a Pro Stock record. She reached a speed of 347 kilometres (215.55 miles) per hour in a race.

Pro Stock engines cannot use turbochargers or superchargers to pump air into the carburetor. That explains the bonnet scoop. It adds power by ramming air into the carburetor. This creates a more explosive air-fuel mix for the engine to burn.

The bonnet scoop makes Pro Stock cars unique.

At a 2013 race, Jirka Kaplan does a burnout in his Funny Car.

FUNNY CAR

Funny Cars are the same size as normal street cars. But their top speeds of more than 507 kilometres (300 miles) per hour are anything but normal. In 2014 Funny Car legend John Force set the fastest mark at just over 521 kilometres (324 miles) per hour.

Funny Cars owe part of their power to their super-fuel – nitromethane. In most Funny Cars, it fuels a 426 Chrysler Hemi engine. A supercharger is mounted on the air intake. This device increases the car's horsepower by 50 to 100 per cent. Funny Car engines can crank out 8,000 horsepower. That is six times the horsepower of Pro Stock dragster engines.

FACT

Some dragsters release parachutes to help slow them after a pass.

TOP FUEL

With their long, wedge shape, Top Fuel cars are the most familiar dragsters. They are also the fastest at the drag strip. Top Fuel dragsters regularly top 483 kilometres (300 miles) per hour. Their unofficial speed has passed 531 kilometres (330 miles) per hour. This explains why racing fans call Top Fuel dragsters the "kings of the sport".

Top Fuellers are about 7 metres (25 feet) long. A tall wing rises in the rear. At high speeds, air rushing over this wing provides downforce. Downforce presses the car onto the drag strip. This gives better **traction** and control. Traction is also aided by super-fat rear tyres, called racing slicks.

TOP FUELLERS: TOP SPEED TIMELINE		
SPEED BARRIER	**DRIVER**	**YEAR**
More than 240 kph	Lloyd Scott	1955
More than 320 kph	Don Garlits	1964
More than 400 kph	Don Garlits	1975
More than 480 kph	Kenny Bernstein	1992

traction grip or friction on a surface

PARTS OF A TOP FUEL DRAGSTER

rear wing

cockpit with roll cage

body

racing slicks

engine

FACT

Racing slicks used by Top Fuel dragsters are more than 25.4 centimetres (10 inches) wider than tyres on normal road cars.

CHAPTER 4

LAND SPEED RECORD BREAKERS

Krr-BOOM! That thunderous jolt was music to the ears of the car crew. They started yelling and cheering. It meant the *ThrustSSC* had just broken the **sound barrier**. Driven by British fighter pilot Andy Green, it was the first car to ever go supersonic. That day in 1997, the jet-powered car also set a land speed record of 1,228 kilometres (763 miles) per hour.

Going after the land speed record is a huge challenge. The cars that try do not look like road cars, race cars or dragsters. They look more like jets or rockets on wheels. In fact, they use jet and rocket engines. These cars have the only engines powerful enough to attempt to set the mark. Experimental vehicles like the *ThrustSSC* take years to design, build and test.

FACT

Most cars pursuing the land speed record use aluminium tyres. Softer, rubber-like tyres can fall to pieces at such high speeds.

sound barrier speed that sound travels

Fighter pilot Andy Green poses next to the jet-powered *ThrustSSC*.

RULES FOR RECORDS

Speed records must meet strict guidelines set by the Federation Internationale de l'Automobile. First, the car must make two passes, one in each direction. This prevents records being set because a car is going downhill or has help from the wind. Second, the car must do the two passes within one hour of each other. That prevents teams from taking advantage of changes in weather or other conditions. The official speed is the average of the two passes.

FACT

The "SSC" in *ThrustSSC* means "supersonic car".

CARS WITH INTERNAL COMBUSTION ENGINES

Normal road cars are powered by internal combustion engines. They burn fuel inside the engine. The crankshaft and other parts transfer the fuel's power to the wheels. Until the mid-1940s, internal combustion engines were the most powerful type of engine available for a car.

In 1947 Briton John Cobb drove his car 636 kilometres (394.196 miles) per hour. It was the last time a combustion engine car set the land speed record. Getting tyres and a transmission that could handle the speed was harder than building the engine.

FACT

The Boeing 747 jumbo passenger jet cruises at 988 kilometres (614 miles) per hour. The airspeed record is 3,529.6 kilometres (2,193.2 miles) per hour. It was set by the SR-71 US spy plane in 1976.

A Chevrolet Corvette Turbo-Jet 360 horsepower engine

JET-POWERED CARS

Jet engines send aircraft screaming through the air. They also sent the *ThrustSSC* to the land speed record of 1,228 kilometres (763 miles) per hour in 1997. Jet engines generate unbelievable amounts of power. *ThrustSSC*'s engines were measured at nearly 110,000 horsepower!

Jet engines use spinning blades to compress air. The air is blended with fuel. When touched by a spark, the mix blasts out of the engine nozzle. The vehicle is then pushed in the opposite direction.

WHERE RECORDS ARE BROKEN

Only a few places on Earth meet the needs for testing land speed records. The surface needs to be flat and hard. The area needs to be big and wide open in case an accident occurs. *ThrustSSC* set its record in the Black Rock Desert in Nevada, USA. Many records have also been broken on Utah's famed Bonneville Salt Flats.

The Bonneville Salt Flats are a perfect place for pushing speed to the limits.

ROCKET-POWERED CARS

In 1970 a car called *The Blue Flame* set a new land speed record. The long, missile-shaped machine was powered by a rocket engine. It reached just over 1,015 kilometres (630 miles) per hour. *The Blue Flame* still holds the record for a rocket-powered car.

The Blue Flame blazes its way to a new land speed record in 1970.

Rocket and jet engines are similar. Both create force by shooting burning gases through a nozzle. But jet engines suck in air to burn fuel. Rockets carry their own oxygen tanks. Fuel cannot burn without oxygen. Rockets can be more powerful than jet engines. But they burn fuel much faster than jets do.

Today teams around the world are racing to build the next experimental high-speed cars. Some of the people who created the *ThrustSSC* have been working on *BloodhoundSSC*. This car uses both a jet and a rocket engine. *BloodhoundSSC*'s goal is to go 1,609 kilometres (1,000 miles) per hour on four wheels.

FACT

In October 2013 American Jessi Combs reached 708 kilometres (440 miles) per hour in the jet-powered *North American Eagle*. She is the fastest woman in the world.

GLOSSARY

accelerate increase speed

aerodynamics science of how objects move through air

carburetor engine part that mixes air and fuel

class category or group

engineering design and construction

horsepower unit for measuring an engine's power

nitromethane mix of nitric acid and propane gas used as fuel in some dragsters

open-wheeler race car built with the wheels outside of the main body; F1 cars and IndyCars are open-wheelers

reliable steady, dependable

sound barrier speed that sound travels

straights long, straight part of a racetrack between turns; cars reach their highest speeds on the straights

traction grip or friction on a surface

FIND OUT MORE

BOOKS

Cars, Trains, Ships and Planes (Visual Encyclopedia), DK
   (DK Children 2015)

Fantastically Fast Cars (To the Limit), Jim Pipe (Franklin
   Watts, 2014)

Fast Cars (It's All About...), Kingfisher (Kingfisher, 2016)

WEBSITES

F1 in Schools
www.f1inschools.co.uk/

Guiness World Records: Speed
www.guinnessworldrecords.com/speed

How Stuff Works: Fast Cars
auto.howstuffworks.com/10-fastest-cars-in-the-world.htm

COMPREHENSION QUESTIONS

1. How might a car's shape affect its speed?

2. Why might one type of race car have wings while others don't?

3. In what ways do you think cars may be different in 50 to
   100 years?

INDEX